CONNECT

Nidhi Datta

BlueRose ONE
Stories Matter
New Delhi • London

BLUEROSE PUBLISHERS
India | U.K.

For permissions requests or inquiries regarding this publication, please contact:

BLUEROSE PUBLISHERS
www.BlueRoseONE.com
info@bluerosepublishers.com
+91 8882 898 898
+4407342408967

ISBN: 978-93-5819-991-8

Cover design: Muskan Sachdeva
Typesetting: Pooja Sharma

First Edition: December 2023

Acknowledgement

Dear Maa – Paa...

I extend my heartfelt gratitude to the two remarkable individuals who have been my unwavering pillars of support throughout my life's journey - my beloved parents, Ma and Pa.

You are, without a doubt, the creators of my being. Your enduring presence during both the peaks and valleys of my life has given me strength, courage and the assurance that I am never alone. Your teachings of ethics and values have been my guiding light, helping me navigate even in your absence.

I am aware that there were moments when I fell short of your expectations, yet you showered me with unconditional love and togetherness. This love became the wellspring of my inner strength, the foundation of my ethics and the driving force behind my spiritual exploration. Your unwavering encouragement and inspiration have allowed me to evolve and grasp the profound meaning of life.

In a world where taking charge of one's life can be a daunting task, your nurturing upbringing equipped me with the understanding of our eternal existence. Your resilience in the face of life's adversities served as a beacon, igniting the spark within me to seek the best possible way to extract the maximum from this existence.

Your dedication to shaping your children into capable individuals, despite the hardships you encountered, has been a testament to your love and determination. You, Ma and Pa, have been the wind beneath my wings.

It took time for me to fully appreciate the zeal that you both possessed, even amidst adversity. Your example has shown me that life is meant to be lived to its fullest, extracting every drop of essence it offers.

I extend this dedication to all those who, like me, wish to explore their hidden potential and maximize the benefits of their existence. Just as knowing how to drive empowers us to overcome hurdles and reach our destination, understanding life skills equips us to navigate any situation that comes our way.

Let this book be a guide for those who seek to connect with their core and grasp the beauty of this precious life.

With boundless gratitude and love,

Nidhi...

Author Introduction

Life, they say, is a relentless teacher. It first administers the tests and then, in its own cryptic way, imparts the lessons. Throughout my journey in this tangle of existence, I've crossed a landscape riddled with highs and lows, experiences that have etched indelible marks upon my soul. Some of these moments have been exquisitely beautiful, while others have been pivotal, altering the course and purpose of my survival.

In the early chapters of my life, I bore witness to circumstances that imprinted a stark truth into my consciousness: things aren't handed to us on a silver platter. To attain anything worthwhile, one must be prepared to wage a relentless battle against adversity. I encountered hardships that tested the limits of my endurance. Yet, with the passage of time, I came to realize that every trial was there for a reason.

As I matured, I became engrossed in the pursuit of both personal and professional endeavors. I believed that I had weathered the worst of life's storms, that the path ahead would be relatively smooth. Little did I know that life had a different script in mind. Challenges persisted, questioning my worthiness and the very essence of my existence. Sometimes, when you're diligently treading the path of righteousness, unaware of your missteps and still confronted by obstacles, you begin to question yourself. I gave my all to both my personal and professional life, yet contentment remained an elusive dream.

Amidst the tumultuous landscape of competition and ambition, the Almighty bestowed upon me the gift of motherhood. This new chapter in my life reshaped my perspective. I began to empathize with the concerns my parents had expressed for me during my formative years. Life evolved, experiences shifted, but adversity remained a constant companion. I found myself wondering if perhaps my life was meant to be a never-ending battle. The routine of existence became my comfort zone and I labored to make it a welcoming abode for my children. Unbeknownst to me, life was preparing me for a grander purpose, one I had yet to fathom.

No matter how many times I faltered or felt disheartened, an external force always seemed to guide me towards safety and self-improvement. My family became an unwavering source of support, rallying behind me through every trial. My parents, my brother, my sister, friends and well-wishers played pivotal roles during my most fragile moments. I navigated the most precarious phase of my life with their unwavering assistance.

During that time, I absorbed life-altering lessons that transformed me. I became an apprehensive and vulnerable mother, but the circumstances demanded that I take charge of my destiny, hold my head high and embrace everything that came my way. I accepted the challenge and charted a new course.

A period of turmoil tested the foundations of my marital life, but it indicated a new beginning. I embarked on a fresh journey with my children, bolstered by my family's steadfast support. I swiftly regained my footing and regained my vitality. In the ensuing years, I invested in self-improvement, striving to unravel the underlying reasons behind life's events. I adopted an aerial view of life, discovering that we possess the agency to sculpt our own narratives. The hardships I endured, I now recognize as blessings in disguise.

As I look back upon the tapestry of my life, I am transported to moments both joyous and harrowing. My memory retains the emotions that infused those experiences, not because of a keen recollection of details, but because those moments were lived with such intensity. There were times when minor victories filled me with boundless joy and situations where I emerged gracefully from profound setbacks. Through it all, I have gathered the fundamental attributes for navigating the web of life.

I write this book with the intention of imparting the wisdom I've garnered, in the hope of nurturing humanity with the skills needed to lead lives filled with joy and grace. If my words can illuminate a path for even a single reader, I will consider my efforts invaluable. You may resonate with some of my perspectives and diverge sharply from others, but I encourage you to delve into the core essence of each idea, to introspect and seek a deeper understanding. I believe that by connecting with the soul of this book, you will feel its vibrations, which can aid in your personal growth and journey through life.

Remember, difficulties do not arrive in our lives to annihilate us; rather, they appear to reveal our concealed potentials. Let adversity know that we are, indeed, the more formidable force.

Why – 'The Connect'

"Why" is a profound and fundamental question that serves as a cornerstone of human curiosity, understanding and purpose. Let's explore its meanings and significance:

1. **Clarity and Understanding:** By explaining the meaning and significance of "why," individuals can gain a clearer understanding of the concept. Clarity is essential for effective communication and comprehension.

2. **Contextualization:** Describing "why" in context helps individuals see how it applies to various aspects of life. Understanding its relevance in different situations can encourage people to ask meaningful questions and seek purpose.

3. **Motivation:** Explaining the importance of asking "why" can motivate individuals to be more curious, introspective and purpose-driven in their lives. Understanding the benefits of seeking reasons and motives can inspire personal growth and achievement.

4. **Encouraging Reflection:** A description of "why" can prompt individuals to reflect on their own lives and actions. It encourages self-examination and introspection, which are valuable tools for personal development.

5. **Facilitating Communication:** When people have a shared understanding of the concept of "why," it becomes easier to engage in meaningful conversations about goals, motivations, values and purpose. Effective communication is essential for building connections and relationships.

6. **Guiding Decision-Making:** Understanding the role of "why" in decision-making helps individuals make more informed and purposeful choices. It empowers them to align their actions with their values and goals.

7. **Inspiring Exploration:** A description of "why" can inspire individuals to explore the deeper layers of their own motivations and the world around them. It encourages intellectual curiosity and the pursuit of knowledge.

8. **Encouraging Philosophical Inquiry:** "Why" questions often lead to philosophical and existential inquiries about the meaning of life, ethics and personal values. Describing "why" can prompt individuals to engage in philosophical discussions and introspection.

In essence, describing "why" serves as a guide to help individuals navigate the complexities of purpose, meaning and motivation in their lives. It offers a framework for understanding the deeper aspects of human existence and encourages individuals to explore these profound questions for personal growth and fulfilment.

Reading "**The Connect**" is an enriching journey that delves into the profound importance of asking "why" in the context of human connections and relationships. This book not only encourages introspection but also offers valuable insights into how understanding the motives and purposes behind our interactions can enhance the quality of our connections with others. It provides a roadmap for fostering meaningful relationships, empathetic communication and a deeper sense of purpose in our interconnected world. By exploring "why" in the context of human connections, "The Connect" invites readers to embark on a transformative exploration of self and others, ultimately leading to more fulfilling and purpose-driven relationships.

Contents

Chapter 1

Understanding Mind, Body and Soul

The tapestry of human existence is intricately woven from three fundamental threads: Mind, Body and Soul. To embark on a profound exploration of life, it is imperative to first grasp the profound significance of these three vital constituents that compose the essence of our being.

The Significance of Mind, Body and Soul

The Soul as the Driving Force

The Soul, the first fundamental aspect of our existence, represents our deepest essence and spiritual core. It is intimately connected to the Divine or the Universal Source, from which it derives its divine qualities and creative power. Much like a drop of water in the ocean shares the characteristics of the vast sea, the Soul shares the inherent abilities of the Almighty. It possesses the power to shape its life and manifest its desires, as it is, in essence, a co-creator of its own life experiences. The Soul embarks on a profound journey through life, selecting a specific life plan that includes a series of experiences, challenges and lessons. These experiences are not arbitrary but are carefully chosen to facilitate the Soul's growth and self-discovery.

In the ancient text, the Bhagavad Gita, it is stated:

नैनं छिन्दन्ति शस्त्राणि नैनं दहति पावकः।
न चैनं क्लेदयन्त्यापो न शोषयति मारुतः॥

This verse conveys that weapons cannot harm the soul, fire cannot burn it, water cannot wet it and wind cannot dry it. The Soul remains invulnerable, eternally connected to the Almighty or the Supreme Universal Power. As an inseparable part of the Divine, it possesses the inherent ability to shape its life and manifest its desires. In essence, our Soul mirrors the omnipotence of the Almighty.

The Soul's purpose is to experience its inherent magnificence and the Divine, despite its boundless capabilities, yearns to understand itself through physical embodiment. Thus, the Soul selects a life plan and embarks on a journey in the material world.

Every experience the soul encounters, whether joyful or painful, is a part of its spiritual evolution.

You may ponder why, if given the choice, a Soul would opt for a life filled with difficulties, sorrows or pain. This question is profound and its answer lies in recognizing that every experience a Soul undergoes on this earthly plane is, at its core, a spiritual one. While some experiences may appear unfavourable or painful in our human perspective, they hold equal spiritual value for the Soul.

Consider the analogy of an actor. An actor derives joy from portraying various characters and testing the limits of their acting prowess. They relish the challenge of embodying diverse roles, whether it be the romantic hero, the menacing villain or the comedic genius. A truly versatile actor can seamlessly transition between roles, earning acclaim for their ability to excel in any character portrayal.

From the soul's perspective, there is no "good" or "bad" experience; all experiences are opportunities for learning and growth.

For instance, when a person faces betrayal, it's not a punishment from the universe; rather, it's a role the soul has chosen to understand the depths of trust and betrayal. When one endures illness, it's an opportunity to explore the facets of resilience, vulnerability and the appreciation of health.

In much the same way, our Soul plays different roles in the grand theatrical production of life. Each role is an opportunity for the Soul to extract profound insights and emotions. The Soul seeks to understand how it feels to bask in the warmth of love, to endure the sting of betrayal, to grapple with illness, to shoulder the weight of debt or to suffer through any other earthly tribulation. Every experience, whether joyous or agonizing, is a facet of the Soul's quest for self-discovery. It immerses itself in the human experience, living every moment according to its chosen life plan, until it deems the essence of that experience fully extracted, at which point it either evolves to a new experience or departs the material world.

Observing life, we often encounter individuals who seem to leave this world for no apparent reason, peacefully transitioning in their sleep, while others experience dramatic transformations. Someone born into poverty may rise to become a celebrated figure on a national scale. Those afflicted with seemingly incurable illnesses may miraculously regain their health. Individuals wounded by life's minor slights can rise to achieve remarkable feats. These occurrences unfold in accordance with the Soul's plan and its inner calling. When the Soul senses that its time in a particular experience has reached its zenith, it forges new paths, guided by its own innate wisdom.

A soul's versatility is measured by its ability to navigate through various life situations, extracting the essence of each experience. When the soul believes it has learned all it can from a particular experience, it moves on to the next chapter of its journey.

Exploring the Mind as the Software of the Self

The mind serves as the software of our being, akin to an operating system driving a computer. It is a dynamic landscape of thoughts, beliefs, emotions and perceptions, continuously evolving as it adapts to new experiences and information.

Understanding the Mind

Distinguishing the mind from the brain is essential. While the brain is a tangible organ responsible for processing information, the mind exists as an ethereal realm where thoughts, beliefs, emotions and consciousness reside. It wields the power to shape our perception of reality and plays a central role in our lived experiences.

The Illusion of the Mind

The mind is often compared to an illusion because it possesses a unique ability to present the duality inherent in the world. Duality involves the coexistence of opposites, such as good and evil, happiness and sorrow and light and dark. This duality is not a quirk of the mind but a fundamental aspect of existence. It serves as the backdrop against which our experiences gain depth and meaning.

The Role of Beliefs and Perception

The subconscious mind operates discreetly in the background, molding our reality based on the beliefs and perceptions it holds.

From birth, we embark on a lifelong journey of acquiring beliefs and forming perceptions. These mental constructs become the foundation of our subconscious mind and influence how we perceive ourselves, others and the world around us. A child's upbringing, in line with their soul's plan, leads to the adoption of a particular belief system. These early influences set the stage for the foundation of one's reality.

Creating Mental Receptors

Our minds function as receptors, attracting or repelling aspects of life based on our beliefs and perceptions. Each individual possesses unique mental receptors, similar to tuning forks resonating with specific frequencies. For instance, someone with a "wealth receptor" naturally attracts opportunities, resources and experiences leading to financial success. Conversely, those without such receptors may struggle to accumulate wealth despite access to the same external resources.

The Body as the Gateway to the Human Experience

The human body acts as the conduit between our inner world and the external reality we inhabit, serving as the tangible vessel through which our souls engage in the multifaceted human experience.

The Body's Resilience Amidst Vulnerability

Our physical bodies, like all living organisms, are not immune to the passage of time, wear and tear and the potential for illness. They adhere to the natural cycle of life, beginning with birth, progressing through growth and maturation and concluding with mortality. This inherent fragility is a universal reminder of our shared humanity.

However, within this fragility, the body exhibits a remarkable capacity for resilience. It possesses an innate ability to heal, adapt and rebound in the face of adversity. Whether recuperating from injuries, battling illnesses or recovering from emotional wounds, our bodies demonstrate an extraordinary talent for rejuvenation and recovery, underscoring the intricate design of the human form.

The Body as the Portal to Sensory Experience

Our bodies are not passive vessels; they are the gateways through which we engage with the richness of the material world. Through our senses—touch, taste, sight, hearing and smell—the body connects us to the diverse array of sensations life offers.

- Touch allows us to connect with the physicality of existence, enabling us to feel the warmth of an embrace, the coolness of a breeze and the comforting pressure of a hand on our shoulder.

- Taste invites us to savor the myriad flavors and textures the world presents, from the sweetness of ripe fruit to the savory complexity of a well-prepared meal. The exquisite taste of a favourite meal can trigger joyful memories, impacting our culinary preferences.

- Sight enables us to witness the beauty, diversity and wonder of the external world, from the grandeur of nature to the intricate creations of art. The sight of a breath-taking sunset inspires awe and appreciation for natural beauty.

- Hearing grants us access to the auditory tapestry of existence, from the emotive melodies of music to the comforting voices of loved ones. The soothing sound of ocean waves induces calmness and influences our choices for peaceful getaways.

- Smell immerses us in the diverse aromas of the world, from the freshness of blooming flowers to the earthy scent of rain-soaked soil.

These sensory experiences leave indelible imprints in our memory, forming the foundation of our future responses. The body's ability to perceive pleasure and pain becomes the cornerstone of our decision-making process, aiding us in navigating the complex and dynamic world we inhabit.

In essence, our bodies are not passive observers but active participants in the human experience, allowing us to fully immerse ourselves in life's richness. They enable us to taste the sweetness of joy, feel the depth of sorrow and partake in the full spectrum of sensations and emotions. Recognizing the profound significance of our bodies enriches our understanding of the intricate harmony of mind, body and soul, guiding us toward a more profound and meaningful existence.

The seamless coordination of mind, body and soul forms the very essence of our existence. Together, they create a unique human experience, with the mind shaping our thoughts and beliefs, the body connecting us to the physical world through our senses and the soul guiding our journey of self-discovery and growth. This intricate interplay between these three elements enriches our existence, providing profound meaning and purpose to our lives.

Chapter 2

Harmony among Mind, Body and Soul

The interaction of mind, body and soul forms a dynamic and influential relationship that shapes our human experience. Our mind serves as the bridge between the physical and the spiritual, interpreting the body's sensations and communicating with the soul's aspirations. Our body acts as the canvas where these interactions manifest, translating thoughts and emotions into actions and reactions. Simultaneously, our body's senses connect us with the external world, which influences our mental and spiritual states. The soul, our eternal essence, provides purpose and meaning to our lives. When these elements are in harmony, we experience alignment, purpose and fulfilment, while neglect or discord leads to imbalance and disconnection. Recognizing this interplay encourages us to nurture each facet for a holistic and enriched human experience.

Beliefs and Conditioning Impact on Health

Our physical well-being is influenced not only by food and water but also by the beliefs and conditioning we absorb throughout life. The connection between mind and body, often referred to as the mind-body connection, demonstrates how thoughts, emotions and beliefs directly affect our physical health. Stress, anxiety and negative emotions trigger the release of stress hormones like cortisol, impacting our immune system and cardiovascular health. In contrast, positive beliefs promote well-being.

Beliefs about health, illness and our bodies significantly shape our physical condition. Strong belief in the body's healing ability can accelerate recovery, while negative beliefs can manifest or perpetuate health issues.

The placebo effect illustrates the profound influence of belief on the body's healing processes and the nocebo effect highlights the opposite outcome due to negative expectations. Conditioning from society, culture and family influences our lifestyle choices, including diet, exercise, sleep and stress management. Recognizing and challenging limiting beliefs through mindfulness practices empowers us to enhance our health and resilience.

Acknowledging the wisdom of the body is essential, as it communicates its needs and imbalances through symptoms and sensations. Paying attention to these signals helps identify areas where beliefs or conditioning negatively impact health. Listening to our bodies and addressing these issues fosters better physical and emotional well-being, promoting holistic health.

Attaining Equilibrium and Harmonization

Achieving balance and alignment among the mind, body and soul is a profound journey of self-discovery and holistic well-being. This integration fosters a fulfilling, purpose-driven life.

- **Mind:** Balance in the mind involves self-awareness and effective management of thoughts and emotions. Practices such as mindfulness and meditation enhance awareness and guide thoughts positively.

- **Body:** Physical health forms the foundation for balance and alignment. Prioritizing exercise, nutrition, sleep and stress management promotes holistic well-being. Practices like yoga and tai chi enhance the mind-body connection.

- **Soul:** Nurturing the soul involves introspection, contemplation and seeking meaning beyond the material world through practices like meditation, prayer and nature connection.

The journey begins with self-awareness, identifying areas requiring balance. Prioritizing well-being involves caring for physical health to support a healthy mind and soul. Mind-body practices and exploring one's life purpose and values contribute to alignment with the soul. Stress management and continuous growth are crucial in the ongoing process of achieving and maintaining balance and alignment.

Attaining harmony among the mind, body and soul leads to greater self-awareness, purpose and fulfilment. This integration empowers individuals to live in harmony with themselves and the world, enriching the human experience.

Nurturing Your Inner Connection

Nurturing your inner connection is essential for achieving balance and alignment among your mind, body and soul. This inner connection acts as a bridge between the physical and spiritual self, promoting harmony and purpose. Here's a detailed exploration of how to nurture this connection:

- **Self-Reflection and Mindfulness:** Allocate regular moments for self-reflection and mindfulness to delve deep into thoughts, emotions and inner experiences. Self-reflection aids in understanding values and identifying imbalances, while mindfulness fosters presence and reduces past regrets and future anxieties.

- **Meditation and Contemplation:** Incorporate meditation and contemplation into your daily routine to connect with your inner self and explore meaningful aspects of life, such as purpose and values.

- **Nature and Solitude**: Spend time in nature and embrace moments of solitude to reconnect with the essence of life and facilitate introspection.

- **Connection with Others**: Cultivate meaningful relationships to enhance self-understanding and recognize the interconnectedness of all living beings.

- **Mind-Body Practices**: Engage in mind-body practices like yoga, tai chi, or qigong to integrate physical and spiritual aspects. Develop heightened body awareness, paying attention to sensations, tension and relaxation.

- **Creative Expression**: Use creative outlets, such as art, writing or music, to deepen your connection to your soul's essence.

- **Gratitude and Service**: Practice gratitude to focus on positive aspects of existence and engage in acts of kindness or volunteering to align actions with inner values.

- **Emotional Intelligence**: Enhance emotional intelligence by becoming aware of emotions and their impact on thoughts and behaviour.

- **Observing Thought Patterns**: Recognize recurring thoughts, beliefs and self-talk, reframing or releasing thought patterns that no longer serve you.

- **Conscious Living**: Live intentionally, making choices aligned with values and purpose and being present in each moment. Explore practices that expand awareness beyond the self, fostering interconnectedness with all living beings and the universe.

- **Seeking Knowledge**: Cultivate a thirst for knowledge and personal growth by reading, attending workshops and engaging in conversations that broaden perspectives. Pay attention to communication, practicing active listening and conscious word choice to foster meaningful connections.

Cultivating awareness and consciousness leads to a more intentional, meaningful and harmonious life, deepening understanding of oneself and the world and achieving greater balance and alignment among the mind, body and soul.

Chapter 3

Unleashing Hidden Potential

This Chapter offers you a comprehensive roadmap for tapping into your hidden potential. It encourages you to explore your inner reservoir, overcome limiting beliefs, view challenges as opportunities and embark on a transformative journey of self-discovery. By embracing these principles, you'll not only unleash your hidden potential but also set yourself on a path toward a more fulfilling and purpose-driven life.

The concept of hidden potential sets the stage for understanding and unlocking one's untapped capabilities. In this section, you'd introduce the idea that each person possesses reservoirs of talents, strengths and abilities that they might not be fully aware of or haven't yet harnessed. Hidden potential refers to the unexplored capacities within individuals that, once identified and nurtured, can lead to personal growth and achievement. This overview aims to create awareness about the transformative journey ahead and motivate readers to explore their inner resources. It's an invitation to embark on a voyage of self-discovery and self-improvement by acknowledging the existence of latent abilities waiting to be unleashed.

Tapping into Your Inner Reservoir

Unleashing your hidden potential is alike drawing from a deep, untapped reservoir within your being. It's a journey that begins with self-awareness and the recognition that you possess untold capabilities waiting to be harnessed. This reservoir isn't limited to a specific skill or talent; it encompasses your creativity, determination, resilience and the power of your mind. To tap into this wellspring of potential, start by quieting the noise of external influences and delving inward.

Engage yourself in self-exploration through introspective practices like journaling, meditation or self-assessment exercises. This will help you identify your passions, strengths and areas where you can excel.

You can reflect on what truly ignites your passion and sense of purpose. Identify the activities or pursuits that make you feel most alive and fulfilled.

Take stock of your existing skills and talents and consider how they can be applied to different aspects of your life. Begin by making a list of your skills, talents and areas of expertise. These can include technical skills, soft skills, hobbies and personal interests. Reflect on what you enjoy doing and what you excel at. Often, skills acquired in one area can be transferred to create success in another. Also be open to acquiring new skills or improving existing ones. The ability to adapt and learn new things is a valuable skill in itself and can be applied across various domains.

Understanding your core values is fundamental to harmonizing your latent potential with the trajectory of your life. Your values serve as a compass, guiding your choices and actions in a way that resonates with your true self. When your aspirations and endeavors are in alignment with your values, you not only harness your hidden potential but also cultivate a sense of purpose and authenticity. It's a powerful synergy that allows you to navigate life's complex terrain with clarity and integrity, ensuring that your journey is not just successful but deeply meaningful. So, take the time to identify your core values and weave them into the fabric of your ambitions and decisions, for in this alignment lies the key to a purposeful and fulfilled life.

Recognizing and Overcoming Limiting Beliefs

Unshackling Your Potential

Overcoming limiting beliefs is a pivotal journey in personal growth, as these deeply ingrained beliefs act as insidious barriers that restrict our full potential. These self-imposed limitations can be thought of as invisible chains that hinder progress and personal development. To embark on the task of unshackling yourself from these mental constraints, self-awareness is key. It involves a multi-step process of identification, questioning, replacement and reinforcement.

1. Identification of Limiting Beliefs: Unmasking the Barriers to Your Potential

The journey to overcome limiting beliefs begins with the essential first step: identifying these self-imposed constraints. Limiting beliefs are those deeply ingrained notions that lurk within our psyche, subtly impeding our personal growth and progress. They tend to manifest during moments of self-doubt, when the fear of failure grips us, or when negative self-talk dominates our internal dialogue. This step is all about developing a heightened sense of self-awareness, becoming acutely mindful of when and how these thoughts surface in your mind. The process is akin to turning on a light in a dimly lit room to expose the lurking shadows. By identifying these limiting beliefs, you're shining a light on the barriers that have been holding you back, bringing them out from the shadows into your conscious awareness. This recognition not only enables you to see them clearly but also provides you with the power to confront and address them directly.

When you doubt your abilities, whether in your career, relationships or personal pursuits, you may not always immediately recognize it as a limiting belief. It might feel like a fleeting moment of insecurity or self-criticism. However, these are often signs that a deeper belief is at play, one that is restricting your self-confidence and potential. The fear of failure can similarly manifest in various ways, from procrastination and avoidance to self-sabotaging behaviours, all stemming from an underlying belief that success is unattainable. Negative self-talk, characterized by self-deprecating thoughts and harsh self-criticism, is another tell-tale sign of limiting beliefs in action.

Becoming acutely aware of these moments, as they happen, empowers you to pinpoint the exact instances when these limiting beliefs are active. It allows you to dissect the thought patterns and narratives that are holding you back. With such awareness, you can confront these beliefs directly, challenging their validity and dismantling the power they hold over your actions and decisions. This process of identification serves as a crucial turning point on your path to personal growth, marking the moment when you decide to no longer let these limiting beliefs control your life.

2. Questioning the Validity of Limiting Beliefs: Demolishing the Illusory Walls of Self-Doubt

Having successfully identified those limiting beliefs that have woven themselves into the fabric of your consciousness, the journey to overcome them advances to a pivotal stage: questioning their validity. This step calls for a probing inquiry into the very essence of these beliefs, urging you to scrutinize whether they stand on the bedrock of concrete facts or are merely frail assumptions. These self-imposed limitations, often veiled as unshakable truths, can, upon closer inspection, reveal themselves to be mere phantoms conjured by your imagination. Through this objective evaluation, you embark on the process of unravelling the intricate mental barriers that these beliefs construct.

In questioning the validity of these limiting beliefs, you essentially cast a discerning eye on the foundation they rest upon. Many a time, these beliefs have stealthily infiltrated your psyche and wrapped themselves in the guise of undeniable certainties. For example, a belief that you're not worthy of success may appear as an irrefutable fact, despite being constructed on subjective perceptions and past experiences. By subjecting these beliefs to the light of scrutiny, you start to dismantle their façade, revealing the fragile scaffolding that supports them.

As you delve deeper into this self-inquiry, you may come to the realization that these limiting beliefs lack substantial evidence, standing as unsubstantiated constructs that have held sway over your choices, actions and self-perception for far too long. By questioning their validity, you don the mantle of a critical thinker, capable of discerning between genuine impediments and illusory walls of self-doubt. This transformation from unquestioning acceptance to a vigilant scrutiny of your beliefs opens the gateway to liberation from these mental constraints, paving the way for profound personal growth and self-discovery. It marks the point where the walls of your self-imposed limitations begin to crumble, revealing a path to a brighter, less restricted future.

3. Replacement with Positive Affirmations and Constructive Self-Talk: Forging a Path of Empowering Transformation

Once the fortress of limiting beliefs begins to crumble under the weight of scrutiny and critical examination, the transformation journey takes a decisive turn towards renewal and empowerment. The third step, essential in this process of self-liberation, is the art of replacement with positive affirmations and constructive self-talk. This stage entails filling the void left by the disintegration of those self-imposed myths with affirmations, which serve as the keystones of your belief system. These affirmations are purposefully crafted statements, each bearing the weight of your belief in your inherent capabilities and boundless potential.

Repetition becomes your closest ally in this quest for internal reformation. By consistently and fervently reinforcing these affirmations, you initiate a profound rewiring of your mental framework, steering it toward a growth-oriented mindset. The transformation that unfolds is not an exercise in indulging in ungrounded optimism, but rather a deliberate and conscious choice to redirect your focus. This redirection guides your mind to place its spotlight on your strengths, the myriad possibilities that stretch out before you and the illuminated path towards your aspirations.

In essence, this step in the journey signifies the recalibration of your inner compass. It entails training your mind to believe unwaveringly in your capabilities and the immense capacity you possess to surmount challenges, break through barriers and transcend the limitations that once seemed insurmountable. It's the moment when you cease to be a prisoner of self-doubt and instead emerge as a conscious architect of your own destiny, fashioning it with the bricks of self-belief and the mortar of constructive self-talk. The process acts as a potent catalyst, sparking the fire of self-assurance and illuminating the way forward towards a brighter and more fulfilling future. As the chorus of these positive affirmations reverberates within, it not only shapes your self-image but also fuels your resolve to stand resilient in the face of adversity, knowing that your capabilities are your allies on the journey to self-realization.

4. Visualization Techniques for Reprogramming the Subconscious: The Power of Mental Blueprints

As the journey to break free from the shackles of limiting beliefs unfolds, the fourth pivotal step ushers in the profound potential of visualization techniques to reprogram the subconscious mind. These techniques constitute a potent means to transform aspirations into reality. They involve the vivid and deliberate act of mental imagery, wherein you immerse yourself in the experience of success, the realization of your boundless potential and the triumphant attainment of your most cherished goals.

Visualization is far more than a mere exercise; it serves as a wellspring of unwavering motivation and a cornerstone of reinforcement. Its primary function is to keep you in alignment with your loftiest aspirations, making them tangible and vivid in your mind's eye. With each dedicated visualization session, you embark on a remarkable journey of self-realignment, ensuring that your actions and decisions align seamlessly with your envisioned success.

This is not an arbitrary exercise but a calculated reprogramming of the subconscious. The images and scenarios conjured during visualization sessions serve as the architects' blueprints for your path ahead. As you consistently and vividly visualize your success, your subconscious undergoes a subtle yet profound transformation. The seeds of belief, sown through each visualization, take root, anchoring themselves in your psyche. They quietly but persistently whisper to your subconscious, convincing it to embrace your envisioned success as a forthcoming reality. These visualized blueprints direct your thoughts, actions and responses with a singular purpose: the manifestation of your dreams. In essence, they become the compass guiding your journey, ensuring that each step is a deliberate stride toward the realization of your full potential.

It's not merely daydreaming or fantasy; it's the cultivation of a mental landscape that mirrors the heights you aspire to reach. With each session, you strengthen your resolve, embolden your determination and light the way with the beacon of your visualized achievements. This process empowers you to infuse each action, no matter how mundane, with the energy and purpose of your envisioned success. The journey of transformation turns abstract desires into concrete goals and the weight of your aspirations finds a firm foundation in your subconscious. In this profound act of self-empowerment, visualization techniques are the architects of your destiny, constructing a bridge between the realm of dreams and the landscape of your accomplishments.

In essence, recognizing and conquering limiting beliefs is a transformative journey that requires dedication and a strong commitment to self-improvement. By embracing this journey, you empower yourself to break free from the self-imposed chains that have held you back. You unlock your hidden potential and gain the ability to achieve what you may have once considered impossible. The process is not instantaneous, but with continuous effort and self-belief, you can steadily dismantle these barriers and reach new heights in personal growth and achievement.

Transforming Challenges into Opportunities: The Art of Thriving Through Adversity

At its core, the art of transforming challenges into opportunities is a fundamental life skill that has the potential to propel individuals toward personal growth and development. Challenges, often looming like formidable obstacles on the path of life, need not be met with anxiety; rather, they can be harnessed as catalysts for transformation. The key to this profound metamorphosis is a shift in perspective, a transformation of one's outlook on adversity and setbacks.

Foremost in this transformative journey is the cultivation of resilience, an unwavering attribute that can significantly alter the way challenges are perceived. Instead of being sources of despair, challenges can be viewed as opportunities to fortify one's character. It's imperative to understand that setbacks are not abnormalities but rather integral components of the journey. They offer lessons and experiences that, when harnessed effectively, become stepping stones that propel individuals forward on their paths of self-discovery and achievement. To embrace challenges is to embrace the transformative power of adversity.

Furthermore, at the heart of this transformation is the embracement of change and adaptability as essential life skills. Life is a dynamic and ever-evolving journey, often punctuated by unforeseen hurdles. The ability and willingness to pivot and adjust one's approach in response to these obstacles can turn seemingly insurmountable barriers into strategic stepping stones toward personal and professional goals. This spirit of adaptability allows individuals to face challenges not with fear but with resourcefulness and a more positive outlook.

Anchored deeply in this process is the fostering of a growth mindset, a powerful cognitive tool for transforming challenges into opportunities. Belief in one's capacity to learn, evolve and adapt is the cornerstone of this mindset. It encourages individuals to approach challenges with an air of curiosity and a keen willingness to learn from each experience. Challenges, when viewed through the lens of a growth mindset, become exciting opportunities to expand one's skill set and knowledge. These obstacles are not impediments but rather gateways to becoming more resourceful and capable individuals. In this way, challenges are not merely navigated more effectively but individuals emerge from the crucible of adversity as stronger, wiser and more resilient beings.

Ultimately, the art of transforming challenges into opportunities is a profound way to not only overcome adversity but to thrive in the face of it. It is an affirmation that within every challenge lies the potential for growth, learning and personal development. With resilience as the guiding star, adaptability as the compass and a growth mindset as the driving force, individuals can navigate the most arduous of life's challenges with a sense of purpose, not as victims of circumstance but as architects of their destinies. In this way, challenges cease to be roadblocks; they become, instead, the very milestones of a fulfilling and triumphant journey through life.

Empowering Your Journey of Self-Discovery

Empowering your journey of self-discovery is a profound and ongoing quest that ultimately leads to a life of authenticity and alignment with your innermost desires and values. This transformative journey is about navigating through the layers of your identity to find your true north and crafting a life that resonates with your genuine self. The foundational step in this voyage is gaining clarity on your core values and principles. These values serve as a compass, providing direction for your choices and actions, helping you lead a more purposeful life driven by what truly matters to you.

A crucial element in self-discovery is identifying and passionately pursuing your interests. When you engage in activities that genuinely inspire and excite you, you're more likely to unlock your hidden potential. By immersing yourself in these passions, you unearth talents and strengths you might not have known existed. These discoveries further enrich your sense of self and contribute to your journey of personal growth.

Moreover, self-discovery is about connecting your actions with a profound sense of purpose. When your pursuits align with your purpose, every endeavour becomes a meaningful step on your journey. You start to see the bigger picture and how your unique path fits into the broader tapestry of life. This connection to purpose infuses your actions with meaning and fuels your determination to live an authentic and fulfilled life. In essence, empowering your journey of self-discovery is an empowering and deeply rewarding endeavour, one that leads to a life shaped by your true self, driven by your passions and enriched by your connection to a meaningful purpose.

Chapter 4

Crafting the Life You Desire

Setting Clear Intentions and Goals

Crafting the life, you desire begins with setting clear intentions and goals that align with your values and aspirations. Intentions are the compass that guides your actions and goals are the milestones that mark your progress. This chapter explores the importance of intention-setting and goal-setting as foundational steps in manifesting your dreams.

Clarity of Purpose embodies the fundamental concept of introspection and self-discovery, encouraging individuals to embark on a profound journey into their innermost aspirations and values. It urges people to meticulously examine their desires and distil them to their very essence. This process is similar to mining the foundation of one's being, stripping away superficial desires and societal expectations to reveal what genuinely holds significance. The intention is to align one's aspirations with their authentic self and the principles that define them. In this context, authenticity denotes the purest representation of one's identity, unclouded by external influences. True purpose emerges when these genuine values and intentions interlace, giving individuals a compass by which to navigate their lives. This clarity of purpose serves as a guiding light, enabling people to make decisions, set goals and pursue paths that resonate deeply with their innermost selves, fostering a more fulfilling and meaningful existence.

The concept of SMART goals is a powerful framework that enhances the process of setting and achieving objectives. It encourages individuals to craft goals that are Specific, Measurable, Achievable, Relevant and Time-bound, which collectively form the SMART acronym. Each of these criteria plays a vital role in creating a comprehensive roadmap for personal and professional growth. Firstly, specificity ensures that goals are well-defined and clear, leaving no room for ambiguity. Measurability enables individuals to gauge their progress and success, as it provides tangible indicators to track. Achievability encourages setting realistic goals that can be attained with effort and determination, preventing the discouragement that may arise from aiming too high. Relevance ensures that these objectives align with one's overarching intentions, ensuring that they contribute to the bigger picture of one's life or career. Lastly, being time-bound imparts a sense of urgency and accountability by establishing deadlines, prompting individuals to stay on track and manage their time effectively. In summary, SMART goals act as a structured and practical framework that transforms abstract intentions into concrete action plans, offering a precise and effective path to personal and professional development.

Vision boarding is a creative and effective tool that plays a significant role in the process of personal development and goal setting. It involves the creation of a visual representation of your aspirations, typically on a physical board or in a digital format. This technique enables individuals to articulate and reinforce their intentions and goals in a way that is both tangible and inspiring. By collating images, words and symbols that resonate with their desires and values, people create a vivid and personalized reminder of what they wish to achieve. This visual aid serves as a powerful source of motivation, as it brings the abstract nature of goals into the realm of the concrete and visible.

A vision board helps individuals to vividly visualize their desired outcomes and can be a source of daily inspiration. It serves as a constant reminder of what they are working towards, fostering a sense of commitment and determination. Moreover, the act of selecting and arranging these visual elements can be a reflective and therapeutic process, allowing for deeper self-discovery and clarity of purpose. Vision boards are versatile tools that can be used in various aspects of life, including career, personal development, relationships and health. They provide a structured, yet highly personal, means of translating one's dreams and intentions into a visual representation that can help drive focus, motivation and a sense of achievement as progress is made toward these goals. In essence, vision boarding is a creative and tangible bridge between one's aspirations and their daily life, turning imagination into reality.

Visualizing Your Ideal Life is a practice rooted in the profound understanding of the human mind's capacity to shape reality. This technique is a potent tool for manifesting one's dreams and aspirations. It encompasses the process of conjuring a mental image of the life an individual aspires to lead, replete with all its vivid details and sensory experiences. The essence of this practice goes beyond mere daydreaming; it encourages individuals to immerse themselves in this mental creation, to feel the emotions and to genuinely believe in the possibility of the envisioned scenario. In doing so, visualization taps into the subconscious mind's ability to influence our thoughts, actions and eventually, our external circumstances.

Visualizing your ideal life is comparable to mental rehearsal; it enables you to mentally walk through the experiences and achievements you hope to encounter in reality. This process serves to not only clarify your desires but also to intensify your motivation, making your goals more attainable. When one vividly imagines their ideal life, they are more inclined to set and pursue concrete goals aligned with that vision. Moreover, visualization can boost confidence and self-belief, as individuals come to recognize that their dreams are within reach.

By refining the skill of visualization, individuals can cultivate a sense of determination and focus, improving their chances of success in various facets of life, from career ambitions to personal growth and well-being. In essence, this practice provides a dynamic bridge between the realm of the mind and the material world, turning abstract dreams into actionable objectives and thus, offering a powerful path towards the realization of one's most cherished goals and aspirations.

Mental imagery, or the art of creating mental pictures and scenes in one's mind, is a powerful cognitive technique that can significantly influence one's mindset, behaviour and overall well-being. Engaging in mental imagery exercises involves immersing oneself in a mental experience where you vividly picture and imagine the life you desire. This practice encourages you to delve into the specifics, infusing your mental images with rich details, vibrant colours and even sensory sensations. By doing so, you not only articulate your goals but also make them come to life in your imagination.

Mental imagery is a versatile tool that can be applied to various aspects of life, including personal development, career aspirations, relationships and well-being. When you immerse yourself in these mental scenarios, you foster a stronger connection with your desires, making them feel more tangible and achievable. This process not only clarifies your goals but also ignites motivation, commitment and belief in their attainability. As you visualize your desired life, you can experience the emotions, challenges and successes associated with it, which in turn helps you prepare for and navigate the journey toward your goals.

Mental imagery can boost confidence and self-esteem, instilling a sense of self-belief as you recognize the potential for your dreams to become reality. It serves as a creative and transformative bridge between your inner thoughts and the outer world, turning abstract aspirations into actionable objectives. By incorporating mental imagery into your daily routine, you gain a powerful tool for personal growth and achievement, making your dreams more vivid and within reach.

Emotional connection is a pivotal aspect of visualization that adds depth and resonance to your aspirations. When you attach positive emotions to your visualizations, you are essentially infusing your mental images with a profound sense of joy, gratitude and fulfilment that is intimately linked to your goals. This emotional component significantly amplifies the potential for your goals to manifest in your life.

Emotions are a driving force in human behaviour and when you associate positive feelings with your goals, you are more likely to be motivated, persistent and enthusiastic about pursuing them. This emotional connection creates a powerful feedback loop: as you visualize your desired outcomes and experience the positive emotions they bring, you become more committed to the journey ahead, more resilient in the face of obstacles and more capable of maintaining focus and determination.

Moreover, attaching emotions to your visualizations helps to rewire your subconscious mind in a way that aligns it with your conscious goals. When your emotional state resonates with your vision, your mind becomes more receptive to opportunities and solutions that can help you achieve your goals. It also fosters a sense of alignment between your inner desires and external actions, making it easier to translate your aspirations into reality. In essence, the emotional connection is the secret sauce that can turn a mere visualization exercise into a potent tool for personal transformation and goal achievement.

Consistent practice is the cornerstone of effective visualization and it plays a pivotal role in reinforcing your intentions and maintaining unwavering focus on your goals. Visualization is not a one-time event but a dynamic process that requires regular engagement. When you practice visualization on a routine basis, you create a powerful habit that continually reminds you of your aspirations and keeps them at the forefront of your mind.

The act of regularly visualizing your goals is alike to consistently watering a seed you've planted. Each session nourishes the idea, helping it grow stronger and take deeper root in your consciousness. The more vividly and frequently you can imagine your ideal life, the more ingrained it becomes in your thoughts, attitudes and behaviours. This, in turn, increases the likelihood of it evolving from a mental concept into tangible reality.

Consistency also ensures that you don't lose sight of your goals amidst the distractions and demands of everyday life. It acts as a steady compass that guides your actions and decisions, allowing you to align your efforts with your overarching intentions. Furthermore, regular practice of visualization fosters an enduring sense of commitment and motivation, making it easier to persevere when faced with challenges and setbacks.

In essence, consistent practice of visualization is like a steady undercurrent that propels you towards your goals. It is a disciplined and empowering process that enables you to transform your dreams into achievable objectives, ultimately contributing to a more purposeful and fulfilled life.

Strategies for Manifestation underscores the idea that transforming your aspirations into reality goes beyond mere wishful thinking; it necessitates deliberate and strategic action. This section serves as a guide to introduce you to a set of powerful tools and methodologies designed to aid in the process of manifesting your desires. It emphasizes the importance of combining intention with well-thought-out plans, highlighting that achieving your goals requires more than mere hope or belief.

Manifestation strategies encompass a diverse array of techniques, such as goal setting, visualization, affirmation and positive thinking. These approaches provide structured and actionable steps that can help you move from a state of desire to one of realization. They encourage clarity and specificity in setting your goals, as well as reinforcing these objectives through vivid mental imagery and positive self-talk. By doing so, these strategies enhance your focus and commitment, which, in turn, increases your chances of success.

In addition to internal techniques, manifestation strategies may also involve external actions, such as planning, networking and seeking opportunities. This holistic approach acknowledges that your inner intentions must align with your external efforts. It urges individuals to take responsibility for their desires, proactively shaping their paths rather than passively waiting for opportunities to arise.

In summary, "Strategies for Manifestation" is a call to action, emphasizing the necessity of combining intent with structured and purposeful strategies to realize your dreams. It underlines the idea that turning your intentions into tangible outcomes requires a comprehensive and multifaceted approach, one that blends the power of thought and action to create meaningful and lasting change in your life.

Affirmations are a potent tool for personal development and goal achievement, as they serve as a means to reprogram the subconscious mind in a positive and constructive way. This practice involves the repetition of positive, empowering statements that reflect your desired beliefs, attitudes and goals. By consistently using affirmations, you can align your inner beliefs and thoughts with your aspirations, effectively rewiring your thought patterns and encouraging a more optimistic and self-affirming mindset.

Affirmations operate on the principle that the thoughts we hold in our subconscious mind can significantly influence our actions and the outcomes we experience in life. When you repeatedly recite and internalize positive affirmations, you begin to shift your mindset and outlook towards a more confident and optimistic perspective. This transformation can be instrumental in making your goals feel not only more attainable but also more in alignment with your authentic self.

Furthermore, affirmations can be customized to address specific areas of your life, whether it's building self-esteem, boosting confidence, or fostering a growth-oriented mindset. They can also serve as powerful tools for managing stress, reducing self-doubt and increasing motivation. By effectively communicating your intentions to your subconscious through affirmations, you can catalyse a positive feedback loop, enhancing your self-belief and motivation to take actionable steps toward your goals.

In summary, affirmations represent a proactive and effective means to bridge the gap between your aspirations and your beliefs. They act as a daily reminder and reinforcement of your intentions, promoting a more constructive and optimistic inner dialogue that can significantly contribute to your personal growth and the realization of your goals.

The Law of Attraction is a metaphysical concept that has gained popularity in the realm of personal development and self-improvement. It operates on the fundamental premise that "like attracts like," suggesting that the energy and thoughts you emit into the universe have the power to attract experiences and opportunities of a similar nature. This concept underscores the idea that our thoughts and emotions are not merely internal processes but have a profound impact on our external reality.

At its core, the Law of Attraction emphasizes the importance of maintaining a positive and optimistic mindset. By focusing on positive thoughts, feelings and intentions, you are believed to emit a corresponding positive energy into the world, which can, in turn, draw positive experiences, people and opportunities into your life. It encourages individuals to envision their goals and desires with unwavering belief, as this mental clarity and conviction can act as a magnetic force that aligns the universe in your favour.

Critics often view the Law of Attraction with scepticism, pointing out that it oversimplifies the complexities of life and circumstances. However, proponents argue that it's not about wishful thinking but about aligning your mental state with your goals, which can lead to a more proactive and positive approach to life. The Law of Attraction complements various other personal development practices, such as visualization, affirmations and goal setting, to create a holistic strategy for manifesting one's desires.

In practice, understanding and applying the Law of Attraction involves cultivating mindfulness, focusing on gratitude and maintaining a hopeful and constructive outlook. By doing so, individuals aim to harness the power of their thoughts and emotions to shape a more positive and purposeful life, which can, in turn, draw in experiences and opportunities that resonate with their intentions. Whether one fully embraces this concept or not, it underscores the significance of maintaining a positive and proactive mindset as a key element in achieving personal and professional goals.

A gratitude practice is a transformative approach to personal growth and well-being that emphasizes the importance of acknowledging and appreciating the positive aspects of life, no matter how small they may seem. This practice encourages individuals to recognize and express gratitude for the blessings they already have, whether it's good health, supportive relationships, a fulfilling job, or simple daily joys. The underlying premise is that by actively cultivating gratitude, you can attract even more abundance and positivity into your life.

Gratitude operates on the principle that focusing on the positive aspects of life can shift your perspective, instil a sense of contentment and foster a mindset of abundance. By acknowledging the blessings you already possess, you create a mental state that is more open to receiving and recognizing opportunities and positive experiences. It's as if gratitude acts as a magnet, drawing in more reasons to be grateful and perpetuating a cycle of positivity.

Furthermore, practicing gratitude has been linked to numerous psychological and emotional benefits, including increased happiness, reduced stress, improved mental well-being and stronger relationships. When you make a habit of expressing gratitude, you become more attuned to the present moment and more mindful of the good that surrounds you. This, in turn, can improve your overall quality of life and enhance your ability to cope with challenges.

In summary, a gratitude practice is a powerful tool for personal development that reminds us to count our blessings and appreciate the richness of our lives. By doing so, we create a mindset that attracts more abundance and positivity, fostering a deeper sense of contentment and fulfilment. This practice encourages a shift away from scarcity and towards a greater awareness of the wealth of positive experiences and opportunities that life has to offer.

Keeping a manifestation journal is a valuable and multifaceted practice that can greatly enhance your personal development and goal achievement journey. This journal is a dedicated space for you to record and track your progress, capturing not only your goals and intentions but also your visualizations and reflections on your path to realization.

One of the primary benefits of a manifestation journal is that it fosters clarity. As you articulate your aspirations, you are forced to refine and clarify your objectives. This process helps you gain a deeper understanding of what you truly desire, honing your focus and direction. The act of writing down your goals and visualizations also serves to reinforce them, making them more tangible and substantial in your consciousness.

A manifestation journal also functions as a powerful accountability tool. It encourages you to set deadlines, milestones and action plans, making you more committed to your goals. As you regularly update your journal, you can monitor your progress and celebrate your successes, no matter how small they may be. This can be highly motivating and helps you stay on track, even when faced with challenges or setbacks.

Additionally, journaling offers a space for self-reflection and self-discovery. It provides an opportunity to explore your thoughts, emotions and insights, giving you a deeper understanding of your journey. This self-awareness can be instrumental in uncovering potential roadblocks, limiting beliefs, or self-doubt that might be hindering your progress, allowing you to address and overcome these obstacles.

In conclusion, a manifestation journal is a versatile tool that combines goal setting, visualization and self-reflection. It provides clarity, accountability and a record of your journey, making it an invaluable resource in your pursuit of your desires. It serves as a companion on your personal growth and achievement journey, helping you stay organized, motivated and in tune with your inner self, ultimately increasing your chances of manifesting your dreams into reality.

The concept of taking inspired action underscores the vital role that deliberate and purposeful steps play in the process of manifesting one's desired life. While setting intentions and visualizing goals are crucial initial steps, they are most effective when coupled with tangible actions that bring those visions into reality. This section emphasizes that the bridge between where you are and where you want to be is constructed through conscious efforts and consistent, motivated actions.

Taking inspired action is about translating your aspirations and visualizations into a plan of practical steps that you actively pursue. It involves aligning your daily decisions and behaviours with your overarching intentions, transforming your dreams into concrete objectives. This approach recognizes that the journey towards your goals may not always be smooth and you may encounter challenges or setbacks. Nevertheless, inspired action keeps you focused, resilient and adaptable in the face of obstacles, as you actively seek solutions and opportunities that bring you closer to your aspirations.

Furthermore, inspired action is grounded in the belief that the universe often responds positively to determination and initiative. It's not just about waiting for opportunities to present themselves; it's about creating opportunities through your actions. When you consistently work towards your goals, you increase the likelihood of serendipity, synchronicity and unexpected support that can propel you towards your desired life.

In essence, the concept of taking inspired action combines intention with initiative, encouraging a proactive and empowered approach to manifesting your dreams. It reinforces the idea that personal and professional growth is not merely a result of passive wishing but is primarily achieved through the consistent pursuit of your goals with passion, focus and determination.

Alignment with your goals and intentions is a fundamental principle that signifies the critical connection between what you aim to achieve and the choices you make in your everyday life. It emphasizes the necessity of ensuring that your daily actions and decisions are consistent with your overarching objectives. In essence, this means that every choice you make, no matter how small, should ideally contribute to or, at the very least, not detract from your progress toward your desired outcomes.

This alignment principle is rooted in the idea that success is not merely a result of big, momentous actions but is often an accumulation of countless small decisions and habits over time. It underscores the importance of maintaining a holistic and focused approach to your goals. When your daily actions are in harmony with your aspirations, you create a more synergistic and powerful force, pushing you closer to realizing your dreams.

Moreover, the concept of alignment encourages self-awareness and mindfulness in decision-making. It prompts you to regularly assess whether your choices and behaviours serve your long-term objectives. It may require making adjustments in your routines, habits, or even relationships to ensure that you're on the right path. This self-awareness can help you eliminate distractions, prioritize your time and stay committed to your goals.

In summary, the principle of alignment is a practical and purposeful approach to goal achievement. It recognizes that each choice you make has the potential to either propel you towards your desired outcome or hinder your progress. By striving for consistency between your daily actions and your overarching intentions, you increase your chances of staying on course, making tangible progress and ultimately manifesting your goals and aspirations.

Overcoming Resistance is a crucial aspect of personal growth and goal achievement, highlighting the necessity of addressing inner resistance and self-doubt that often emerges when pursuing one's dreams. This concept acknowledges that the path to manifesting your aspirations is rarely linear and internal barriers, such as limiting beliefs or fear, can obstruct your progress.

Overcoming resistance involves a process of self-awareness, where you identify and confront the beliefs and thought patterns that hinder your journey. These limiting beliefs often manifest as self-doubt, fear of failure, or a sense of unworthiness. By recognizing and acknowledging these obstacles, you can begin to challenge and reframe them. This may involve seeking evidence that contradicts these negative beliefs or actively replacing them with positive and empowering thoughts.

It's essential to remember that overcoming resistance is not a one-time endeavour but an ongoing practice. It requires patience, self-compassion and a commitment to personal growth. By addressing inner resistance, you can fortify your mindset, cultivate resilience and navigate setbacks with a more positive and determined attitude. Ultimately, this process empowers you to overcome self-imposed limitations and forge ahead on your path to achieving your dreams, manifesting your goals and leading a more fulfilling life.

Staying Open to Opportunities is a mindset that encourages individuals to be receptive to unexpected possibilities and serendipitous occurrences that may emerge as they work towards their goals. It recognizes that while setting intentions and taking deliberate actions are crucial, life often presents unforeseen opportunities and synchronicities that can propel one closer to their desired outcomes.

This approach emphasizes flexibility and a willingness to adapt to change. It acknowledges that the path to achieving one's dreams is not always straightforward and that rigidly adhering to a preconceived plan may cause individuals to overlook opportunities that could be even better suited to their goals. Staying open to opportunities means being attuned to signs, coincidences and unexpected connections that may present themselves and being willing to explore them.

Furthermore, it's important to recognize that these unforeseen opportunities can provide unique advantages. They might offer new perspectives, introduce valuable relationships, or open doors to uncharted territories. When individuals remain open to these possibilities, they expand their horizons and enhance their potential for personal and professional growth.

In summary, "Staying Open to Opportunities" is about fostering a mindset that balances goal-setting and intention with adaptability and receptivity. It acknowledges that the universe often provides surprising and meaningful paths to one's aspirations. By embracing this approach, individuals can be more agile and better equipped to seize the opportunities that may unexpectedly come their way, ultimately increasing their chances of achieving their desired outcomes.

Persistence and Patience underscore the vital qualities needed for successfully manifesting one's desires. It acknowledges the fact that the journey towards achieving your goals can often be a gradual and evolving process, not an immediate or linear path. These two qualities, persistence and patience, are the keys to navigating this journey effectively.

Persistence involves unwavering determination and a commitment to your vision. It means not giving up when faced with obstacles or setbacks. It's the understanding that challenges are an inherent part of any pursuit and that overcoming them often requires resilience and the willingness to keep pushing forward. Persistence means repeatedly taking action, making necessary adjustments and refusing to be discouraged by temporary failures.

Patience, on the other hand, is the ability to wait for the right moment and trust in the timing of the universe. It recognizes that manifestation may not always happen on your preferred schedule and that some goals require time to come to fruition. Patience is not synonymous with complacency; it is about having faith in the process, embracing the present moment and understanding that the seeds you plant today may take time to grow.

Combining persistence and patience is a potent recipe for success. It means continuously working towards your goals while also being understanding and accepting of the timing of their achievement. This approach helps individuals stay focused and maintain a positive outlook, even when results are not immediate. By persistently taking action and patiently allowing time for your efforts to bear fruit, you increase your chances of ultimately manifesting your vision and realizing your goals.

This will serve as your guide to crafting the life you desire. By setting clear intentions and goals, engaging in powerful visualization, employing manifestation strategies and taking inspired action, you are equipped with the tools to turn your dreams into reality. This chapter encourages you to become an active participant in your life's creation, empowering you to shape your destiny and manifest the life you truly desire.

Chapter 5

The Art of Coordination

Aligning Your Thoughts, Actions and Desires
Coordination of your thoughts, actions and desires is the cornerstone of achieving your goals and living a fulfilling life. This chapter explores the significance of aligning these three key elements and provides practical insights into how you can achieve harmony among them.

Mindful awareness is the practice of consciously and non-judgmentally observing one's thoughts, feelings, sensations and surroundings in the present moment. It involves cultivating a heightened sense of awareness and attention to the here and now, without getting entangled in past regrets or future anxieties. This practice enables individuals to become more attuned to their inner experiences, allowing them to respond to life's challenges with greater clarity and wisdom. Mindful awareness is often cultivated through mindfulness meditation and other mindfulness exercises, which encourage individuals to anchor their attention on the sensations of their breath, bodily sensations or external stimuli. Over time, this practice can lead to a deeper understanding of one's thought patterns and emotional reactions, ultimately empowering individuals to make conscious choices and manage stress more effectively. Mindful awareness is not only a tool for stress reduction but also a pathway to enhanced emotional intelligence, improved focus and a more profound connection with the present moment and the world around us.

Remember that creating an action plan is a dynamic process. It requires ongoing monitoring and adjustments as you progress toward your goals. By breaking your objectives into actionable steps and following a structured plan, you increase your chances of success and maintain focus on your desired outcomes.

Synergizing Mind, Body and Soul

As elaborated in chapter one, synergy among your mind, body and soul is essential for holistic well-being. This section delves into the integration of these three core components, emphasizing the benefits of balance and alignment.

Mind-Body Connection Understand the powerful connection between your mental and physical health. Practices like meditation, yoga and mindfulness can help you achieve greater harmony between your mind and body.

Nourishing Your Soul Cultivate practices that nourish your soul, such as meditation, prayer or spending time in nature. These practices help you tap into your inner wisdom and intuition.

Holistic Health Prioritize your overall well-being by addressing physical, mental and spiritual aspects of health. A balanced lifestyle that includes healthy habits, stress management and self-care contributes to a harmonious mind-body-soul connection.

Fostering Resilience Life is filled with challenges and uncertainties and making resilience. Develop resilience by reframing adversity as an opportunity for growth. Embrace setbacks as valuable lessons and cultivate a mindset that thrives in the face of challenges.

Adaptability Skills Enhance your adaptability by remaining open to change and new experiences. Embrace uncertainty as a chance for innovation and personal evolution.

Stress Management Learn effective stress management techniques to cope with life's demands. Stress reduction practices, such as mindfulness and relaxation exercises, can help you maintain balance during challenging times.

Mastering the Dance of Life: Life is often likened to a dance, with its rhythm, flow and occasional unexpected steps. This chapter concludes by exploring the art of mastering this dance and navigating the complexities of existence with grace.

Mindful Living Embrace mindful living as a way to stay present and savor each moment. By being fully engaged in the present, you can enhance your overall life experience.

Adapting to Change Embrace change as an integral part of life's dance. When you master the art of adaptation, you can gracefully move through life's transitions.

Balancing Priorities Strive for balance among various life priorities, including work, relationships, self-care and personal growth. Balancing these aspects contributes to a harmonious and fulfilling life.

This is how you can master the art of coordination in your life. By aligning your thoughts, actions and desires, synergizing your mind, body and soul, fostering resilience and adaptability and ultimately mastering the dance of life, you will achieve a sense of balance and fulfilment. This chapter empowers you to live with purpose, grace and resilience, navigating life's twists and turns with confidence and inner harmony.

Chapter 6

Navigating Challenges and Adversities

Navigating challenges is an intrinsic part of the human experience. Life, in its complexity and unpredictability, often presents us with obstacles, setbacks and adversity. How we approach and navigate these challenges can significantly impact our personal growth and overall well-being. It requires a resilient mindset, a problem-solving orientation and the willingness to learn from every experience. Challenges are not merely roadblocks but opportunities for self-discovery and transformation. By facing them head-on, we can harness their potential to enhance our strength, resilience and wisdom. Navigating challenges is not about avoiding difficulties but about developing the skills and mindset to overcome them with grace and determination, ultimately emerging from each trial stronger and more equipped for the journey ahead.

Adversities are the inevitable trials and tribulations that we encounter throughout our lives. These adversities come in various forms, including personal, professional, emotional and physical challenges. They can range from financial hardships and health issues to relationship conflicts and personal setbacks. While adversities are often unwelcome and can bring pain and discomfort, they are an integral part of the human experience.

Adversities test our resilience, character and ability to adapt. They push us out of our comfort zones and force us to confront difficult circumstances. Despite their inherent difficulties, adversities also carry the potential for growth and transformation. Through these challenges, we can discover inner strength, develop coping strategies and gain valuable life lessons.

It's essential to remember that adversities are not insurmountable obstacles but rather opportunities for personal and spiritual development. How we respond to these challenges shapes our character and defines our journey. By facing adversities with courage, determination and a willingness to learn, we can not only endure but also thrive in the face of life's trials.

Transitioning from problems to solutions is a crucial pivot in the journey of personal and emotional growth. While problems may appear daunting and overwhelming, they are, in essence, opportunities for transformation and self-discovery. By shifting our focus from dwelling on the challenges at hand to actively seeking solutions, we embark on a path of empowerment and resilience. This transition marks the moment when we decide to take control of our circumstances and approach them with a proactive and solution-oriented mindset. It is through this shift that we unlock our potential to overcome adversity, find creative answers to complex problems and ultimately craft a life that aligns with our deepest desires and aspirations.

Developing a Solution-Focused Mindset

Life is a journey filled with its fair share of challenges and adversities, some anticipated, others unforeseen. However, what truly distinguishes one individual's path from another lies in their response to these trials. Developing a solution-focused mindset is an invaluable skill that equips us with the tools and outlook necessary for navigating the complexities of life. It is essentially an art, a way of approaching problems with unwavering optimism and a problem-solving orientation. This mindset serves as a powerful beacon that directs our attention away from the often paralyzing act of dwelling on the problem itself and instead urges us to explore and discover viable solutions.

In cultivating a solution-focused mindset, we embark on a transformative journey where we learn techniques to reframe challenges. We discover the art of dissecting these seemingly invincible obstacles into more manageable parts, allowing us to address them step by step. This breaking down of problems into smaller, digestible pieces can make even the most daunting issues appear less intimidating. Additionally, a solution-focused mindset encourages us to tap into our innate creativity, enabling us to unearth innovative and unconventional answers that might have been otherwise overlooked.

The true strength of this mindset lies in its empowering nature. It grants us the courage and determination to confront obstacles head-on, to face them with resilience and a belief that there is a solution waiting to be discovered. Moreover, it fosters an ability to transform setbacks into opportunities for growth. Instead of seeing challenges as roadblocks, we perceive them as chances to learn, adapt and become more robust versions of ourselves.

In essence, the development of a solution-focused mindset is a transformative and empowering journey. It is a philosophy that enables us to transcend the limitations of mere problem recognition, offering a holistic approach to life's challenges. It empowers us to embrace difficulties as stepping stones on our path to success and personal development. Ultimately, it is the key to turning life's adversities into opportunities for growth, resilience and a more fulfilling existence.

Using Difficulties as Catalysts for Growth Challenges and adversities, while frequently unwelcome and even daunting, possess the remarkable ability to act as catalysts for personal and spiritual growth. Rather than shying away from them, embracing these difficulties can lead to profound transformations. When we confront adversity head-on, we are often confronted with our own inner strength and resilience that we might not have been aware of before. These trials have the potential to unveil facets of our character and abilities that were previously hidden, fostering a profound sense of self-awareness.

In the face of adversity, we are pushed to tap into our inner reservoirs of strength, resilience and determination. As we navigate through the storm, we learn to adapt and find new strategies to overcome the challenges that confront us. This process inevitably fosters a profound sense of inner strength that was dormant or overlooked in more comfortable times.

Moreover, viewing challenges as opportunities for self-discovery and personal evolution empowers us to extract wisdom from every experience, no matter how gruelling. Every hardship holds valuable life lessons and insights, often revealing more about our own capabilities, values and priorities. This reframing of adversity as a teacher, rather than a tormentor, allows us to grow and evolve. We become more empathetic, compassionate and understanding, not just towards ourselves but also towards others who face their own difficulties.

Ultimately, by embracing life's challenges as catalysts for personal and spiritual growth, we transform these hardships into stepping stones toward a more enriched and enlightened existence. We become more resilient, self-aware and deeply attuned to the profound lessons that life offers. Instead of being weighed down by adversity, we rise above it, emerging as stronger and more resilient individuals, equipped with a deeper understanding of ourselves and the world around us.

Building emotional resilience is a vital skill that equips individuals with the capacity to navigate life's myriad challenges with grace and composure. In the face of adversity, it is this resilience that allows us to endure difficulties, maintain our mental and emotional well-being and emerge from setbacks stronger than before. To cultivate emotional resilience, one must explore various strategies and practices aimed at bolstering this essential attribute.

Mindfulness practices play a central role in building emotional resilience. By learning to be present in the moment and engage fully with our thoughts and emotions, we become better equipped to handle difficult situations. Mindfulness fosters self-awareness, allowing us to acknowledge and understand our emotional responses. This self-awareness forms the foundation for effective emotional regulation. When we can recognize our emotional triggers, we are better positioned to respond to them with a sense of calm and control.

Stress management techniques are another integral component of emotional resilience. In our fast-paced and often stressful lives, the ability to cope with stress is paramount. Strategies such as deep breathing, meditation and physical exercise can help us manage stress effectively.

By reducing the impact of stress on our emotional well-being, we become more resilient in the face of adversity.

Furthermore, emotional resilience involves the skill of emotional regulation. This means learning how to channel and express our emotions in a healthy and constructive manner. It's not about suppressing emotions but rather acknowledging them, processing them effectively and using them as valuable feedback for personal growth. Emotions can serve as powerful indicators of our needs, desires and values. Learning to harness this emotional feedback loop empowers us to adapt and respond to changing circumstances with a positive outlook.

In conclusion, building emotional resilience is an ongoing process that involves mindfulness practices, stress management techniques and emotional regulation skills. By cultivating emotional resilience, individuals can bounce back from setbacks, maintain a positive outlook and adapt to changing circumstances with greater ease. It allows us to not only endure adversity but also harness it as a catalyst for personal growth and self-improvement. In essence, emotional resilience is a cornerstone of well-being, helping us thrive in the face of life's challenges.

Overcoming obstacles with grace is a reflection of one's character and resilience in the face of life's inevitable challenges. These hurdles are an inherent part of our journey and how we choose to approach and conquer them can greatly define our personal growth and development. This section offers guidance on how to navigate obstacles with dignity and composure, emphasizing the significance of several key attributes.

First and foremost, patience is a crucial virtue when facing obstacles. It entails understanding that solutions may not come immediately and that the path to overcoming difficulties may be a long and winding one. Patience allows us to endure setbacks and delays with equanimity, as we recognize that persistence and time are often necessary components of triumph.

Perseverance is another indispensable quality when encountering obstacles. It involves the determination to keep moving forward despite setbacks and even when the odds seem insurmountable. The ability to stay committed to one's goals, regardless of the challenges encountered, can be a defining factor in success.

Maintaining inner calm is also paramount when dealing with obstacles. Cultivating emotional resilience and the capacity to keep one's cool in the face of adversity can significantly impact the outcome of any challenge. Inner calm allows for clearer thinking and more effective problem-solving, helping us navigate obstacles with a level head.

In addition to these personal attributes, maintaining a positive attitude is a powerful tool when confronted with obstacles. A positive mindset not only helps in maintaining motivation but also contributes to the ability to find creative solutions to problems. Seeking support from friends, family, or professionals can also provide valuable insights and resources to help overcome obstacles effectively.

Staying focused on your goals is the guiding light that can lead you through the darkest of times. A clear sense of purpose and vision can help you persist even when the going gets tough. By holding onto your goals, you maintain the momentum necessary to navigate challenges with resilience and poise.

In essence, embracing an attitude of grace when facing obstacles is an art that combines patience, perseverance, inner calm, a positive mindset and a resolute focus on your goals. It is a testament to one's character and resilience, as it allows individuals to navigate even the most daunting obstacles with poise and unwavering determination. By embodying these principles, one not only overcomes challenges but also emerges from them as a stronger, more resilient individual, better prepared for the journey ahead.

Chapter 6 serves as a beacon of empowerment, offering invaluable guidance on how to navigate the often tumultuous waters of life with wisdom, resilience and grace. It presents a comprehensive approach to not only overcoming challenges and adversities but also leveraging them as catalysts for personal growth. The development of a solution-focused mindset is highlighted as a cornerstone, teaching individuals to shift their focus from problems to solutions, thereby transforming adversity into an opportunity for progress. It emphasizes the importance of using difficulties as a catalyst for personal and spiritual growth, allowing individuals to emerge from adversity stronger and more self-aware. This part also delves into the essential skill of building emotional resilience through mindfulness practices, stress management and emotional regulation, which equips us to endure and rebound from setbacks with composure. Lastly, the chapter touches upon the art of approaching obstacles with grace, promoting patience, perseverance and inner calm in the face of adversity. By embracing these principles, individuals gain the tools and insights necessary to view life's challenges as stepping stones towards a deeper understanding of oneself and a more fulfilling journey through life. It empowers to not only weather the storms of life but to thrive in the midst of them, emerging with greater wisdom, resilience and an enduring sense of inner strength.

Chapter 7

Deepening Your Connection

Deepening your connection is a profound and enriching journey that encompasses various dimensions of human existence. It involves a deep exploration of the self, a nurturing of relationships with others, the quest for meaning and purpose in life and a yearning for a sense of oneness with the universe. This journey goes far beyond the superficial aspects of life and delves into the profound depths of human experience, spirituality and self-discovery.

Firstly, deepening your connection through the profound exploration of the self is a transformative journey of self-discovery. It entails delving into the intricate layers of your thoughts, emotions, desires and values. This process of self-reflection and introspection allows you to go beyond the surface and gain a profound understanding of who you are as an individual. It's a bit like embarking on an expedition into the uncharted territories of your inner world. Through this exploration, you begin to uncover hidden talents and passions that might have remained dormant or undiscovered. You also confront unprocessed emotions, experiences and memories, which, when acknowledged and understood, can lead to healing and growth. This profound journey of self-discovery not only enables you to better comprehend your motivations and aspirations but also empowers you to tap into your untapped potential. As you navigate this intricate inner landscape, you become more self-aware, gaining insights into your strengths, weaknesses and the values that guide your life. Ultimately, deepening your connection with yourself is a voyage of personal growth and transformation, one that equips you to navigate life's challenges with a stronger sense of purpose and authenticity.

Secondly, it involves Nurturing relationships with others is a fundamental aspect of human experience that extends beyond immediate family and friends, encompassing the broader human community. It involves actively and purposefully cultivating meaningful and authentic connections with a wide range of individuals. Deepening your connection with others entails several key components, including building meaningful relationships, fostering empathy and understanding and cultivating a sense of compassion and connection with those around you. These relationships are crucial for emotional well-being and have the power to significantly enhance the quality of your life.

1. Building meaningful relationships involves going beyond the surface level of interactions and investing time and effort into developing deeper connections. This means taking the initiative to get to know people on a personal level, understanding their thoughts, feelings and experiences. It's about creating a sense of trust and openness that allows for genuine and honest communication.

   Meaningful relationships can be formed in various contexts, from friendships and romantic partnerships to professional connections and community involvement. When you invest in these relationships, you create a support system that can enrich your life, offer guidance and provide a sense of belonging.

2. Empathy and understanding are essential components of nurturing relationships. Empathy involves the ability to recognize and share in the feelings of others, while understanding entails gaining insight into their perspectives and experiences. By practicing empathy and understanding, you can build deeper connections with people.

   When you empathize with others, you show them that you care about their well-being and that their emotions matter. This creates a strong bond and fosters trust. Understanding, on the other hand, helps you navigate conflicts and disagreements more effectively, as it allows you to see situations from multiple angles and find common ground.

3. Compassion is a driving force in nurturing relationships. It involves a genuine concern for the suffering and well-being of others. When you practice compassion, you actively support and care for those around you, creating an environment of kindness and mutual support.

   Cultivating a sense of connection means acknowledging our shared humanity and interconnectedness. It involves recognizing that we are all part of the same human experience and our actions and choices can impact one another. This perspective encourages you to treat others with respect and compassion.

4. Being strong and supportive relationships play a pivotal role in enhancing emotional well-being. When you have a network of meaningful connections, you are more likely to experience feelings of happiness, security and fulfilment. These relationships offer a source of emotional support during challenging times and can contribute to a sense of purpose and belonging.

5. The quality of your life is significantly enriched by the relationships you nurture. Whether it's enjoying the company of close friends, finding support from your family, or feeling connected to your community, these relationships provide a profound sense of belonging

and purpose. They offer opportunities for shared experiences, personal growth and emotional fulfilment.

Nurturing relationships with others extends to your immediate family, friends and the broader human community. It encompasses the deliberate building of meaningful connections, fostering empathy and understanding and cultivating compassion and a sense of connection. These relationships are not only essential for emotional well-being but also enhance the overall quality of your life, providing a supportive network of individuals who share in your joys and offer solace during challenging times.

Thirdly, the quest for meaning and purpose in life is an existential journey that lies at the core of human existence. It's a profound exploration into the very essence of your being, a journey to discover what truly matters to you and what infuses your life with significance. This introspective expedition leads you to question the fundamental aspects of your existence, such as your values, passions and the impact you wish to have on the world. It's about seeking answers to age-old questions about the why and how of your existence. What is it that brings you joy and fulfilment? What is your unique contribution to the world? These are the inquiries that propel you on a quest to find your purpose.

Discovering your purpose can have a transformative impact on your life. It provides a compass that guides your choices, actions and priorities toward a more meaningful and fulfilling existence. With a clear sense of purpose, you're no longer adrift; you're anchored by a profound understanding of what you want to achieve and the legacy you wish to leave behind. Purpose doesn't just give you direction; it also offers motivation and a profound sense of fulfilment. It infuses your everyday life with intention and passion, inspiring you to pursue your goals and values relentlessly. The quest for meaning and purpose is a deeply personal and introspective journey, but its rewards are far-reaching. It empowers you to live a life aligned with your true self, where each day is imbued with a sense of significance and fulfilment as you strive to make a positive impact on the world.

Lastly, deepening your connection through a yearning for a sense of oneness with the universe or a higher power is a profound spiritual and philosophical journey that transcends the boundaries of individuality and seeks to understand the interconnectedness of all life. It's a quest to find a deeper sense of purpose within the vast and intricate textile of existence. At its core, this journey is about recognizing that you are not separate from the world around you but an integral part of it.

This quest often involves spiritual or philosophical practices such as meditation, prayer, or a deep appreciation for the natural world. Through meditation, individuals can cultivate a heightened awareness of their inner selves and in doing so, connect with the universal consciousness that unites all living beings. Prayer, in its various forms, provides a means of communication with a higher power, offering solace, guidance and a profound sense of interconnectedness. Nature, with its awe-inspiring beauty and complexity, can be a gateway to feeling at one with the universe, reminding us of the intricate web of life in which we play a unique and meaningful role.

This yearning for oneness with the universe is a pursuit that has been at the heart of many spiritual and philosophical traditions throughout history. It seeks to answer profound questions about the nature of existence and our place within it. The journey towards this sense of unity often leads to a profound transformation of one's perspective on life, offering a broader and more interconnected view of the world. It provides a deep and abiding sense of purpose, as individuals come to understand their role in the grand cosmic design. Ultimately, deepening your connection in this way is a deeply personal and transformative journey that opens the door to a heightened spiritual awareness, a profound sense of purpose and a feeling of unity with the universe that transcends the boundaries of the self.

This is a multi-faceted and enriching journey that spans the realms of self-discovery, human relationships, finding meaning and purpose and seeking a profound connection with the universe. It is a transformative voyage that can lead to personal growth, emotional well-being and a deeper sense of purpose and fulfilment in life.

Chapter 8

Living Your Connect

Living life to the fullest is an aspiration and a journey that encompasses a commitment to embrace every moment, experience and opportunity that comes your way. It's about extracting the maximum value and joy from each day, recognizing the impermanence of life and living with purpose, passion and authenticity.

Embracing Every Moment

Embracing every moment is the essence of living life to its fullest. It signifies a profound connection with the present, a practice of savouring the simple joys of existence and a recognition of the precious gift of being alive. In this approach, each passing moment is viewed as an opportunity to engage with the world in a way that transcends the ordinary and mundane. It is about finding beauty in the everyday, deriving joy from the seemingly insignificant and treasuring the unique experiences life offers.

Chasing Your Passions

Pursuing your passions and interests is a crucial and deeply enriching aspect of embracing life to its fullest potential. At its core, it involves recognizing those activities or endeavors that ignite a profound sense of enthusiasm within you and dedicating your time and energy to them. It's about identifying what sets your soul on fire and allowing that inner spark to guide your choices and actions.

Seeking New Experiences

Embracing life to the fullest hinges on the willingness to venture beyond your comfort zone and actively seek out new and diverse experiences. This endeavour can manifest in a multitude of ways, such as embarking on adventures to unfamiliar destinations, indulging in novel cuisines that tantalize your taste buds, immersing yourself in learning a fresh skill or language, or boldly accepting challenges that stretch your boundaries.

Building Meaningful Connections

Human connection is the emotional cornerstone of a deeply fulfilling life. It revolves around the intricate art of not only building but also nurturing meaningful relationships with those closest to you – your family, friends and loved ones. These connections contribute layers of depth and richness of your life that no material possession or personal accomplishment can ever replicate.

Living with Gratitude

Gratitude, the profound and transformative mindset of acknowledging and appreciating the blessings in your life, is a potent solution that enhances the experience of living life to the fullest. It's a lens through which you view your world, allowing you to recognize and celebrate the abundance that surrounds you, whether those blessings are big and grand or small and seemingly inconsequential.

Balancing Work and Leisure

Achieving a balance between work and leisure is crucial for a fulfilling life. While professional success is important, it should not overshadow your personal well-being and enjoyment of life. Allocate time for relaxation, hobbies and self-care to maintain a healthy work-life balance.

Living with Purpose and Fulfilment

Living Your Connect is about translating the profound insights and practices you've cultivated throughout this journey into a life of purpose and fulfilment. It begins with embracing your unique life purpose, the calling that resonates deeply with your heart and soul. Explore strategies for aligning your daily actions with your sense of purpose, transforming your life into a meaningful and fulfilling journey.

Integrating Mind, Body and Soul into Daily Living

Integration is at the core of living your connect. It's about bringing the harmonious interplay of mind, body and soul into your daily existence. Learn how to synchronize your thoughts, emotions and physical actions to create a life that resonates with your authentic self.

Sustaining Your Connection Throughout Life's Phases

Life is a dynamic journey with various phases and transitions. Sustaining your connection means adapting and evolving as you progress through these stages. Whether you're in the process of career-building, raising a family, or transitioning into retirement, discover the art of resilience, flexibility and mindful adaptation as you navigate the complexities of different life phases while staying true to your core values and purpose.

Leaving a Legacy of Love and Wisdom

Living Your Connect isn't just about personal fulfilment; it's also about leaving a legacy of love and wisdom for future generations. Your deepened connection can inspire and positively impact others. By sharing your experiences, wisdom and values, you contribute to a more compassionate and enlightened world. Explore ways to mentor, guide and inspire those who come after you, leaving behind a legacy that transcends your individual existence.

Conclusion

The Eternal Journey of Connection

In concluding this transformative journey through the realms of Mind, Body and Soul, we arrive at the realization that our existence is a sacred tapestry intricately woven with threads of connection. We have delved into the depths of self-awareness, unearthed the power of intention and harnessed the magic of mindful living. We've navigated the stormy seas of challenges, learning to dance with the adversities that shape our souls. We've celebrated the beauty of unity, both within ourselves and with the world around us.

As we stand at the face of this concluding chapter, it's imperative to recognize that the journey of connection is never-ending. It is an eternal dance, a continuous exploration of the self and the cosmos. It is a commitment to living with intention, to nurturing our inner connection and to embracing the boundless possibilities that life offers.

Our connect with Mind, Body and Soul is not a destination but a perpetual voyage, a cosmic odyssey that transcends time and space. It's a commitment to living life with purpose, authenticity and a deep sense of interconnectedness. It's a recognition that our existence is both a singular thread in the fabric of the universe and a vibrant tapestry woven with the stories of countless souls.

As we take these closing steps in our journey together, may we carry with us the wisdom gained, the connections forged and the intentions set. May we live each day as an opportunity to deepen our connection with ourselves, with others and with the boundless mysteries of existence. And may we leave a legacy of love, wisdom and unity for future generations to inherit.

Remember, dear reader, that your journey of connection is unique and profoundly meaningful. You are the author of your own story, the weaver of your own textile. The pages of your life are waiting to be filled with the colours of joy, purpose and connection.

In closing, I invite you to embrace the eternal journey of connection with an open heart and a curious spirit. May your life be a testament to the power of living with intention, mindfulness and a profound sense of oneness. May you continue to deepen your connection with Mind, Body and Soul, for it is in this sacred interplay that the true essence of life is discovered.

Thank you for embarking on this transformative journey with me. May your path be illuminated with the light of connection and may your heart be forever filled with love, purpose and boundless wonder.

With deep gratitude and infinite connection,

Nidhi....

Milton Keynes UK
Ingram Content Group UK Ltd.
UKHW021156220224
438285UK00006B/65

9 789358 199918